THE WORDS WE WEAR

THE WORDS WE WEAR

New and Selected Poems

GLENDAL WALLACE

ENDICOTT AND HUGH BOOKS

Proceeds from the sale of this book are donated
to the Saint Louis Poetry Center.

Endicott and Hugh Books
P.O. Box 13305
Burton, WA 98013
www.endicottandhughbooks.com

THE WORDS WE WEAR New and Selected Poems

Published by Endicott and Hugh Books, Burton, Washington
www.endicottandhughbooks.com

Book Design: Masha Shubin
Cover Illustration: Stella Levi

ISBN: 979-8-9943445-0-7

Printed in the United States Trade paperback

Endicott and Hugh Books
P.O. Box 13305
Burton, WA 98013
www.endicottandhughbooks.com

CONTENTS

III

IV

V

To my husband William, whose love, patience and understanding eyes helped give these words purpose, place and their wings.

INTRODUCTION

It was toward the end of 2025 that I had the good fortune to read the work of Glendal Wallace. She had been referred to Endicott and Hugh Books by our mutual friend Dr. Rosetta Moore and for me personally, this introduction couldn't have come at a better time. Many of us who were born decades before the sixties have seen remarkable progress validating the belief of Martin Luther King, Jr. that the arc of the moral universe is long, but it bends toward justice. The rights of women, people of color, and the LGBTQ community have advanced to help our country achieve a more perfect union; most of us never believed we would have lived long enough to see a Black president and first lady.

For a country deeply rooted in racism, sexism, homophobia and xenophobia, the decades of progress in our lifetime—although long overdue, gave us hope that this union would only continue to bend toward liberty and justice for all.

But 2025 and now 2026 (the year *The Words We Wear* is published) has brought a regime of brutal cruelty, greed, chaos and corruption. With crushing speed, our government has embarked on the ethnic cleansing of our population and is literally trying to whitewash our history and the voices of people of color. White supremacists are in positions of power. Forces that many of us consider evil are moving to destroy all the progress we had come to cherish. It has made the task of our time the challenge of finding inner peace and joy in our individual lives, while at the same time holding a steadfast commitment not to turn away like the Germans of the 1930's.

The poetry and prose vignettes of Glendal Wallace exquisitely hold this duality; she powerfully writes of what she describes as "the malevolent stench of raw injustice felt by another human being" while other poems reflect her compassion for all people and a transcendent ability to be nurtured by beauty and love. To maintain this duality is an inspiration, and the poetic voice which expresses it is one we need more than ever.

Jeanie Davies Okimoto, Publisher
Endicott and Hugh Books

I

WHERE IT BEGINS

It begins with a child.
Every living soul wears their words
for even a child, an infant who cannot speak
wears their words:

hold me

nurse me

clothe me

protect me

we the old souls exude our words
allude our words, even try to hide
the words we wear but the discerning
mind will see it empathetic heart
will feel it, wise soul will know it.

QUILT-PIECES

Torn little swatches, precious patches
scattered remnants of life creating:
collecting memories is like quiltmaking
each piece connects a particular story
distinct relevance   person   place item
becoming a memory that assembles
in time a mosaic of past present future
taking in
            giving out
                        ahhhhhhhh
collecting memories is like jazz
enhancing new renditions grooves
improvisations that rhythmically journey
becoming one sound that evolves
in time as notes of kaleidoscopic fusion
taking in
            giving out
                        ahhhhhhhh
collecting memories is...
like quiltmaking
                        like jazz
                                    like life
                                                ahhhhhhhhhhhhhhhhhhhhh.

LEATHER BIBLE BELTS

The Midwest
where I grew up
was heavily laced
in leather bible belts
let me tell ya' baby
oooooooooooooooh
you try entertaining
a worldly thought
I mean you just
TRY entertaining
a worldly thought
let me tell ya' baby
oooooooooooooooh
your butt got
guilt-whipped right
from the pulpit.

WHERE MY JEWELS ARE

For the Past Residents of Fillmore, Pierce and Polk Street. The 1960's-2020.

Memories of children
memories of elders
memories of fathers
fathers who wickedly worked
swing-shift hours killing
their swing-shift bodies
in dust ridden
commerce driven
U.S. steel mills
buying their chryslers
chevys buicks and fords
memories of mothers
mothers who cooked
better meals
for other folks
than they did for their own
while playing children
jumped their ropes

Memories of lil' girls
lil' girls who go from being sweet
to sweet lips and wide hips
kissing and rolling those wide hips
with lil' boys in dark
deep dark narrow gangways
memories of lil boys
lil' boys who grew up fast
became grown men—hustling
dreams drugs and dragons

roaming city streets
streets that became
ghost towns when
dust-ridden
commerce driven
U.S. steel mills
LEFT!
That is where
my jewels are
STUCK!
in the squalor
in the familiar *(that keeps us who find comfort)*
surviving, holding on by faith Yes!
I know
the jewels
of this place:
            the life there
            we played there
            lived there
LOVED!
some died there—
but memories
still remain
Stuck!
that is where
my jewels are
Stuck!   Stuck!   Stuck!
            in sidewalk cracks
                        near front porches
            buried in backyards

            hidden in bedrooms
                        under chifforobes
            stacked on shadow boxes
                        perched in church wings
            left in dark alleys
                        rubbled in vacant lots

lots now full—
full of grown trees
trees and old souls
souls and sixty years
sixty years of ALL
ALL my memories
ALL my innocence
memories and innocence
innocence and jewels
jeeeeeeeeeeeeeeewels
jeeeeeeeeeeeeeeewels
jeeeeeeeeeeeeeeeeewels.

THE FORGOTTEN ELDER

He was a gentle man all his ninety years
never dared step on another man's foot
Today he sits
with tired brittle bones he is shaken by
the changing of this new America
the devious words heard on media
corruption seen on sacred grounds
Today he hears
this new America   what it has become
with its...
googles and yahoos
alexas   and   teslas
robotics and 'lectronics
amazons and   pelatons

This forgotten man of ninety years
Today he mourns
for our youth dying daily
on the streets of this new America
for our CEO's
plundering wealth like common thieves
for our leaders
pillaging promises like slimy slumlords
for our cities
becoming wastelands from bureaucratic neglect
            and now he grieves
for victims of greed chaos and incivility
for those deceiving others
while deceiving themselves
oh my, he says
            look at our new America.

THE SHIRLEY THAT I KNEW

Eyes keen as city eagles
wit so sharp
could cut flesh
could fool the wise
with her non
descriptiveness
juxtaposed in
lyrical vignettes
her masterful realism
leisurely woven on
hemlines of prolific
poetry and chenille
laced skirt.

HAIR

Hair is an extraordinarily simple topic. Take my sister Florence. She has never had a bad hair day. None that I ever witnessed in nearly four decades. Her bob-cut, sable brown hair was always professionally styled, neatly coiffed, well managed. Mine. *Lord have mercy.* Wayward strands combed forward the night before ended up laying backwards when I awakened. Pieces that were bone straight converted to crunchy curly fries by the end of the day. My hair has a mind of its own. Period. *Umph.* It doesn't think about, wouldn't consider being managed by any cosmetologist. Not even Colin Powell could manage my hair. No! It takes orders from a higher general. Who? I don't know.

NICE AND SLOW

For DeYonne

Too weak to hold on
too strong to let it go
so Death came quickly
at a pace called Nice and Slow
cancer of strength and fear
spew tumors with no relief
metastasize its strength
at a time of unbelief
now our tears flow like breaths
our memories weave like lace
sustain the strength we have
rememb'ring her dear embrace.

WORDS TAKE THEIR OWN JOURNEY

Like a custom-tailored garment
a quilted piece of clothing...our
words can be worn, communicated
through impetuous action radiated
through mildly compressed inaction
(whether we admit it or not) words
take their own journey and arrive
intact at their nestled destiny with
ease and intent then, they are
indisputably manifest without
saying a word: it is what they exude.

THE NEWS

Don't want your comfort for my tears
it won't bring back his precious years
for he is gone– our Fred is dead
we heard the news that's all we said

not long ago they stomped his face
can only imagine that awful place
where were his friends and did they know
was someone near and did they go

to see his scars hurt me so bad
but he survived for that I'm glad
we went our way for just a while
we left kind words a friendly smile

a year or two I came to learn
that dreaded news my heart would yearn
thought he recouped his many woes
but au contraire' his fatal foes

came in the guise of loveliness
a woman's charm and coy I guess
they shared a passion that turned to greed
their wants transformed into some need

a flow of bullets that took his life
we'll never know the sudden strife
three days went by, his body found
a neighbor thought he was still around

his life was gone– *the blood cried out!*
his life was gone– *bones took a shout!*
he left his hammer that was his tool
he left his style forever cool

puffing his smoke talking his talk
carrying his ladder walking his walk
now he is gone– our Fred is dead
we heard the news that's all was said.

TOOL BOX

I wonder what kind of items my dad
kept in his tool box–
did he house the usual gadgets
hammer nails wrench screwdrivers
sockets and assorted ratchets
that part of his life–
I don't recall
he was more of a lady's man
tools he kept on hand were his
mischievous charm ready smile
engaging thirst silk ties Italian brims
yes the only memory I recall
that 1979 Lincoln Continental
era of him driving "Mr. Towne Car"
one day it needed fixing so he called
a neighbor guy slim-Jim man in his 30's
he took a look at my dad's silver
crown jewel garage-kept automobile
last I heard my dad got scammed
out of hundreds of dollars for repairs
that should've cost a few tens
wish he had his own set of
mechanical skills maybe then–
his tool box
would have come in
handy for his needs
        and the womenfolk.

THE POUND CAKE BATTLE

Moving across the country and living out of boxes can lock your mind up for months. Although my mother had passed away some years ago, I pondered on her essence and wisdom in hopes of remembering where I stored the recipe for her delicious pound cake. What a struggle. When that Sunday morning arrived, we had invited family over so I was preparing to do my pound cake prance. First, I placed six medium eggs and four sticks of butter in a glass bowl to get room temperature ready. After a few moments, I heard my long-time, beige looking mixing bowl chuckle, *"Now you think you gonna bake it like she did? You got another thing coming."* Yes, I was up for the challenge and told this son of a tupperware... *You're on!* As I creamed the butter and eggs into a soft mixture, it began to resemble the exact consistency I'd witnessed as a child when my mother whipped a pound cake together before you could say Sunday School. Then, the struggle came back. I heard that same vexing chuckle trying to upset my flow. *What next? You stuck?* Suddenly I vacillated between how many cups of flour to use. Anyone knows that flour is the foundation of a cake. Was it two cups or four? No. Maybe. Yes. I went with two. Next, I added two cups of sugar. Then, I started feeling my confidence juices from my forehead and the sweat juices from my underarms have their private warfare. I turned the noisy ceiling fan from low to high. It was going to be ME versus this POUND CAKE.

I told myself, Confidence is gonna win this match! I began mixing the creamy and dry ingredients together and got to going...I was wearing my confidence in bold letters. On my printed apron. On the arms of my faded denim shirt. On my flour-dusted fingers. Fear and doubt had stabilized.

Oh, you think you're hot stuff now... I began rigidly blending the mixture with my handmixer...even dropped a dab of vanilla extract and lemon extract in the mixing bowl. Then, I decided to kick things up a notch by squeezing a little juice from a lemon and adding this to the creamy mixture. Oh I was feeling snazzy... then, my mind returned to locked mode and my confidence plundered. Should I add more flour or not? No. Maybe. Stop. I decided to sprinkle about a cup of flour—I didn't measure— my mother never did. Suddenly, her words of wisdom quietly, unerringly spoke to me...*"A burnt child dreads fire...but always put on courage when you need it."* I whipped and stirred then whipped some more. The batter was coming together nicely. My mother would approve. I greased and floured my metal bundt pan—the kind that lifts right out the middle so you can sit the cake on a fancy, floral dinner plate to let it cool. Next, I wiped that smirk right off the side of my mixing bowl. I tilted and wobbled the bowl as I poured the batter so the sides would fill up evenly in the pan. Like my mother did. The oven was hot and waiting for my cue... Once out the oven, I delivered a moist, "*Shut your mouth*" golden brown pound cake to my house guests. The sparring match was over. Gloves off and wiped clean. My wrists and fingers were ready for serving. After dessert, there wasn't a slice left.

SOCIETY'S GARDEN

I am a custom-made trellis
entwined in society's garden
of childhood memories and
adult realities whose sanctum is
interwoven vines of weeping and
wailing—for our elders and children
for what their eyes have seen
hearts have felt, hands have
touched. Alienation and abuse
shellacked with lies and laughter
revealing a trussed latticework of
festive foulness and lost innocence.

MEN AND MEDICINE

It's funny how conversations go through transformation given time and history. There used to be a time when I (like most young people) was considered to have issues. Now I have topics. Ease upon any dialogue where older folk are chatting and you'll hear topics ranging from the weather and health to politics and the news. Topics. Not so when you're young. You spend your time yakking about social media, how to make a living, how to get rich quick, relationships and men. Yes, MEN. But, when you get older, you sit around and talk about medicine. What's hurting, how long it's been hurting and what you're taking for the hurt.
Medicine. Not men.
No, menfolk conversations
become reserved for young and brazen women who have...
the energy to engage in emotional gymnastics and still...
tolerate the drama and strain of relationship goals.

WE WEAR OUR WORDS

We wear our words
whether soft
and silent
perhaps seductive
whether mild
and mellow
perhaps mischievous
whether rich
and raw
perhaps raging
nonetheless
we wear it
               it shows.

CREATE

to cause
to come into being
like God did in
genesis chapter 1
causing light moon stars heavens
seas rivers mountain plains
EARTH
to stretch forth:
Yes, creativity at its finest!
What does man create:
test-tube fertilization
robotic machination
electric car automation
gene cloning simulation
AI generation...?
Must crack God up.

BENEFITS AND BURDENS

My words may neatly rhyme
or wildly roam free
they do not fold or gently close
no harm they give you see

soft spoken vibrant words
sit quietly on this page—
their only thought disparage not
mere syllables of a sage

slim stanzas of violet and velvet
maroon from age and time
not pale and meek but dark and deep
occasional blends of rhyme

these words collect no dust
nor harbor bookshelf rows
they speak with grace in every space
with utterance that flows

quick jaunts of joys and pleasure
may catch you unaware
not always sweet—but still a treat
benefits and burdens I share

so hear my words oh listener
they're crystallized tears
that echo worlds from ancient pearls
a cistern full of years.

POETING A POEM

Oh, it's tough
nowadays
to poet a poem
birth words
utter words
uncensored
    undressed
        unbanned

words that come
out of your
deepest self
you see:
groans
    moans
        oooooooohs
            ahhhhhhhs
                Mymymys
                    Lord have mercies
get in the way.

DUE SEASON

One year I spent time in the southwest Illinois region. When I first arrived, there was a broad piece of farmland directly outside our condo. The area was dry and desolate with scattered rows of dead branches. Pretty much like my writing motivation at the time. Stuck and without any sign of productivity. Zilch.It reminded me of what the prophet Ezekiel perceived as a "valley of dry bones."

That was during the month of April...

Three months later and that same bereft cornfield became filled with vivid lush cornstalks. Rows and rows of tall healthy green stems as far as eye can see. Amazing.

What did it mean?

It symbolized the simple essence of faith.
I must write.
Regardless of my level of motivation. We all go through tests and life lessons. It is during those times that circumstances may lack any hope promise or sign of life. Much like that cornfield. Yet, at the right time... in "due season" we are able to reap a bountiful harvest of opportunity and expectancy if we remain focused, faithful ... and never lose heart.

HEART AND CRAFT

For Toni Morrison

Your fingers of organic insight
sew keenly written words
on the fabric of history's
embellished bedspread
you expose patriotic
toxic quilt-pieces,
stitched and stenched
senseless atrocities
horrific inadequacies
Then,
you rewrite our perceptions
in spectacular Nobel splendor.

I DREAM OF WORDS

I dream of words:
not quietly studied
like a raveled piece
of saddle tan carpet
on a living room floor
not shamefully frozen
in a pool of muddled
water filled with late
fall leaves
not compromised
covered with mothballs
in a basement cedar chest
no,
I dream of mighty words
released
fitly spoken
having their say
vesseled
placed in deep vats
slooooooooooooooooooooooooooooooooowly
fermented…
distilled…
in aged oak
enjoyed at the right time.

HEADSPACE

Shall I cruise to Aruba
sparkling sizzling azure waters
gently tumble over in layers
fluff like carefully battered meringue
sweetly rise and turn and rise
sweetly rise and turn and rise

Shall I
Shall I

Shall I return to Curacao
island of trading slaves
evolve your Dutch
with vibe-filled roads
rural ragged rough
exchanging *dushi*
for new diamond watches
while commerce spends
like factory swatches
Sweetly rise and turn and rise
Sweetly rise and turn and rise

Shall I
Shall I
What shall I do?

Dushi: Creole-Caribbean language for "everything that is sweet."

HAWAIIAN SAMPLING

Hush
                Hush
                                Hush
lush
green
golden
forests
sway like obedient choirs

lush
green
golden
palm trees
fan their slender fingers
whispering praise

lush
green
golden
ferns
wave rambling hands
with joyful certainty

Hush
                Hush
                                Hush.

ALOHA MORNING

Majestic succulents
swift-moving geckos
take morning peaks
tropical rains refresh
intermittent souls
with liquid joy
docile volcanic lava
spilled from a once
forceful eruption
now a stately summit
host to mountain climbers
paying homage to
an Aloha morning.

HOMELESS

Nimitz Avenue near Honolulu Airport

We
leave by shuttle
6:05 a.m.
tottle around
airport detour
We
and gray crisp skies
greet his spastic eyes
willow wild hair
bare
feet
swinging hands
pecking
pecking
pecking
traffic buttons
for sport.

HOMELESS II

#42 Bus route on Nimitz Ave, Honolulu-Hawaii

Ash and sores blotch black
sun-kissed ankles matted hair
he sleeps   bent   no home

PEARL HARBOR

deep dark memories
release Pacific waters
fleet flows waters mourn

....

flag sways somber hands
USS Arizona
sunken ship aged tears

THE GRAND CANYON

time cannot kill earth cannot
steal sacred ground dances
like quiet strength

....

mountain shadows come
heal our hearts from vast divide
light we need each tribe

SAGUARO AND SEDONA

dust sanctuary
prickly arms elevate
like green desert angels

Sonoran desert grain
golden cacti grow
beauty speaks in silence

one touch of Sedona
you feel warm goodness
of God's magnificence

Sedona's aura crystal
glowing, vortex moving
nature's landscape

red rocks host grandeur
while distant chants, humble
knees on chapel rock pray

LOVERS IN A JAPANESE GARDEN

For Doris and Joseph

Weeping willow
drops along an
evening lit koi pond
wisteria climbs gracefully
lovers renewing wedding vows
while joyful tears sparkle
under a near clear sky
mandolin music blends
from a distant path
bystanders clutching glasses
sipping on magical notes
from hope, sake
and evening air.

LOVE DESERVES

To frolic through luscious green parks
hurriedly flowing city streets gaze at
beautiful castles whose beauty fails to
compare to newly wedded bliss to magically
stop—and give each other that look of love
Yes love deserves…
to swirl aimlessly, skipping to sounds of morning
birds, scurry along cast iron fences listen to nature's
melodies then stop—at whim—to sit on steps of
contemplation pondering, waiting its next move
Oh yes, love deserves…
despite seasons of sadness sickness stale days
despite plateaus of poverty perplexity painfulness
despite egresses of injury injustice indecency, despite
treading cobblestones of chaos conflict cultural
divides, despite tumbling down rolling meadows of
misery misfortune malice
Love still deserves…
to believe all things hope all things endure all things
So yes, let love dance—it must
lift its limber arms in praise and adoration
victoriously glide along streets of faith
sprinkled with mercies surprises passion
yes, let love exude its breathful aura
whisper its tender request
close its eyes
give warm kisses
ooze its playful pheromone
wiggle its feet *(if it wants)*
for love deserves its dance.

THE PRIVATE STRUGGLE OF SOCIAL DISTANCING

We dwell in loneliness
from an unseen enemy
homes locked in grief
fears placed on shelves
like store-bought groceries
for commonplace relief
living in sanitized safety
our pseudo subtle faces
portray a masked shame
with nondescript smiles
that hide our fear with
dichotomy and game
what glory see the world
our outer text beholds
while occupied within
collects our tortured souls.

TWISTED

Transforming changing evolving
life has a way of reshaping us
making us fit *(in our circumstances)*
some call it finding your niche
your place so we change
in and out
we evolve up
and
down
back
and forth
transforming.

This corona virus has
transformed us
conformed us
informed us
and yes
deformed us
I see the look of
twistedness
on our faces.

LIFE'S LEAVES

Scattered here
scattered there
all around the ground
fallin amidst our days
restless senseless nights
life's leaves are a fallin'
we never know the turns
they're takin'when
circumstances come a callin'
down
down
down
red
        as city violence
green
like corporate corruption
orange
        as prison jumpsuits
sporadic
        as government functions
I said,
red
as city violence
brown
like Uvalde pain
fragile
        as immigration
sudden
        like Camp Mystic rain

life's leaves are a fallin'
we never know the turns
they're takin'when
circumstances come a callin.'

CONFUSION

Water reflects our face
life reflects our heart
all we see today
changes before it starts

lies and propaganda
flourish with ease
state laws are tying hands
INFLUENCE is the new disease

mental illness is out of control
everywhere it shows its face
when they put 'em back on the street
they turn around and shoot up the place

politicians say this is right
next day say this is wrong
conveniently changing their minds
to whatever wind's blowin' strong
taxes ever rising
little man pays through the roof
while government investigations
go away with just one poof

balls of confusion
balls of confusion
tumbling, tumbling down
whirling our minds
into mass delusion
spinning round and round

rich men live as kings
homeless live as dirge
public aid is all a joke
lobbyists are ever scourge

some preaching love
others teaching hate
with gun violence in the streets
ev'ryone becomes live bait

'bortions, books and bans
surge daily in the news
lil Johnny still can't read
no matter what words we choose

AI is now on the scene
its revolution growing strong
what's real vs. what's fake
what's right vs. what wrong

when life's balls start to settle
and ethics fall into place
what judgment will be rendered
will show on everyone's face

balls of confusion
balls of confusion
tumbling, tumbling down
whirling our minds
into mass delusion
spinning round and round.

URGENCY

Help!
I am looking through a periscope of loss
and deficits reflecting inhalations
intubations, postulations while days
transform from nonsense newsbriefs
celebratory chaos to shaping
semblance out of that which blurrrrrrrrrrrrrrrrrrrrrrrrrrrrrrrrrrrrrrrrrrrrrrrs
my reality:
science vs. propaganda
reality vs. AI
logic vs. foolishness
fluid vs. metric
analog vs. digital
respect vs. buffoonery
power vs. corruption
nation at risk vs. nation at war
truth vs. error
Help!

THE NEW BUSINESS MODEL

Where entrance
to an ethereal world
of unguarded greed
is the goal.

TO THE MAKERS OF FICO*

I applaud you
O creators of FICO
with your clever systems of advantage
your risk protection strategies
you. are. everywhere.
cloaked in fine sheepskin
you witty imperialists
you wall street magicians
you shape new ideas
of trickery treachery slavery
ALL in the name of a credit score.

* *standard credit score*

FILTH

At its best,   filth…
(like comfort) is a state of being
a designated place
growth mindset.   Filth may lie
somewhere between
powerlessness and powerfulness…
between states of oblivion and
domains of self-absorption…
between escapism and undeniable
bondage.

Filth degrades, impairs, plunders the mind.
Be it the woman who is dying and
chooses to stay endeared to a week-old
plate of decomposed dinner scraps
left lying on the floor of her mitigated
bedside. Or the man plagued by
prostate cancer who sips ice to give him
daily comfort while foregoing medical
treatment to stay alive.   Consider the man
who works in an executive office charged
to make executive decisions choosing
rather to behave like a baseline imbecile
fixated on power and ambition.
This too is filth.

VICTIMS

Ukrainian diaspora
witnessed in real time
invoking
ebullient amounts
of currency
mass meetings
mass media
mass millions
flowing carrying delivering
sentiment sympathy succor
for its victims:
men women children

African diaspora
witnessed in reel time
wretched slaveships

strapped trapped cramped
'crossing pernicious waters

flowing carrying delivering
floggings beatings whippings
for its cargo:
men women children

how will we aim to
help the cause of
prevent the death of
force the end of
stop the sale of
men women children
victims too

Who will approach

the podium the airwaves the courts
the media the world
call it crimes
against humanity
what if what we had
we have again today
who or what
would intercede?

WORDS OF OUR CHILDREN

Lives of Camp Mystic
become statistic when swept
by a river's wrath

Holding empty pots
we cry starved and left to die
in a war's bloodbath

Sweet flesh of young girls
to be spiced and spread anew
groomed for lustful path

Who will guide us to
the door of truth who will
protect us from harm?

Where is our place
where are our sentinels
who will guard our choices?

WORDS OF OUR CHILDREN II

snatched   displaced
are   the words we wear
severed from Love
feeling only despair

cry   cry   cry
who will hear our tears
walls   thick as Death
cage   our hopes and our fears

does the world feel our pain
does its eargates hear our cries
we are hearts of helpless children
scorched by Hate's   senseless lies

CONGOLESE RIDDLE

Where are the precious hands*
of innocent Congo children?
They are buried in red rubber's treasure chest.

* *The hands of many Congolese children had been cut off as part of punishment and used to enforce the quota production of rubber in the Belgian Congo. This took place from 1885-1908.*

NEW RAISIN IN TOWN

The old one dried up
festered
big time
eventually
EXPLOOOOOOOOOOOOOOOODED

Or
returned to its
unceremonious
1960's
underrepresented
neighborhood

Well
how come this old one
had to return to
its ol' stomping ground

Yet
how come this new one
had to get **ANOTHER** raisin
to cover for it
how come this new one
had to remove
any semblance of itself
this new one
had to pretend
it's NOT new
had to pretend
it's NOT a raisin

had to acquiesce
its texture
its flavor
its taste
its color

had to pretend
it has NO raisinness-like qualities

had to slough
rid its normal pathological process
rid its normal appraisal process

had to strip its
take down its
shed its.
cleanse its
whitewash its
raisiness-like qualities
to have hope
a better life?

WHAT I AM NOT

I am not your boy
your girl incarcerated
segregated suffocated
by your lawless legislation
void of policies and bills
designed to protect me
your manifest destiny
on my neck so cruelly
I am not your benefits
and burdens of unfair
distribution your invisible
man woman employee
who sits with you
but you don't see me
whose voice is not heard
opinion not acknowledged
name not spoken
application not read
because you deem
I have no worth

I am not your strange fruit
ripe peach dried raisin
snatched property stolen
chattel whose only role
is to acquiesce my being
to your comeuppance

I am not your redlining
undefining gerrymandering
fear pandering
to eventually become
your voter-less entity

I am not your subject
of ongoing disparity
your thesis of popularity
O say can you see?
No that won't ever
work for me
So take your tired
your poor your wretched
misconceptions your
driving miss daisy who
chauffeurs through madness
scuttles through crazies
your blissful world
of dickinson poems
walden ponds
transcendental speech
that sells no bonds

For I am not your drug
medicated for your
clarity propelled by
your pity I am not
your nursing home
corona grown statistic
your pipelined crop shipped
to a manufactured shop
whose only task is
working in fields of pain
and punishment while
you profit from your
rules and regulation

I am not your
lesson before dying
I shine too.

WARNING

This poem contains content
that may be disturbing
may look *suspicious*
while walking
          while jogging
                    while shopping
                              while driving
while
breeeeeeeeeeeeeeeeeeeeeeeeeeeeeeeeeeeeeathing

may disregard your neck
while s t   r   e   t   c   h e d
your
head
held
high
your
hands
raised
up
your
feet
placed
firmly
on the ground
This poem was not there
but it was there
it may be   pulled   a   p   a   r   t
          or
                              pulled over
for questioning   may be found
                    GUILTY

for disturbing the peace
when there was
NO PEACE
This poem
may shake it
may shake it to the east
shake it to the west
shake it to the one
that you love best

This poem
shrieeeeeeeeeeeeeeeeeeeeeeeeeeeeeeeeeeeeeeeeks
from mothers
fathers
sisters
brothers
This poem HURTS
from being
'buked and scorned
with kneeeeeeeeeeeeeeeeeeeeeeeeeeeeeeeeeeees
on its neck
its neck
its neck
while s t r e t c h e d
But this poem *looooooooooooooooooooooooooooooooooves*
your neck
your neck
your neck
while PROUDLY
s t r e t c h e d
even if THEY
don't
love it.

JOLT

Nothing like a jolt to get you going. Moving. Out of a situation. Relationship. A city, a chair or simply out of bed. Jolts. Glad we have them. Some days and in some situations we not only need a jolt…we need a bolt to strike us. **A jolt is not enough!**

Been in situations and places where the jolt <u>was</u> a bolt. Thank God. Saved my butt. Saved my life. When I "look back and wonder how I got over." That old hymn is ever true. It wasn't just my soul but my mind, my body and my tailbone… Jolts compel us. Constrain us. Urge us on. Get us going. We need them! Otherwise...we lay up... lay back...lay around…spend wasteful, nonproductive hours in a mental wasteland. Aren't you glad to get that jolt?

WEEP AMERICA–THE DIRECTIVE

We are a nation who must find our way
until we do we shall weep:
yes America weeps
she releases her tears in the same place
she deposits her memories marinated
from our streets, schools, institutions
our government, clergy, our courts
our cities, homes and
our hearts.

She feels the change but
America is stuck
what does she do with the pain, the tears
(the memories) does she store them in vials
ban them from history books
un-chisel them from public statues

plummet them in diaspora waters or
must she empty herself like an
apothecary's ashes?

yes America is stuck
stuck between her beauty and her vile
between her comfort and her filth
between her poverty and her greed
STUCK

between democracy and lawlessness
between humanity and bigotry
between compassion and brutality
STUCK

between history and heresy
between literacy and blindness
between truth and utter deception
STUCK

and so she weeps.

IV

GO STAY I WONDER

Is there such a place
where words
what people cannot say
GO
what people do not say
STAY
these words
what people will not say
I WONDER
words of
fear
shame
disbelief
anger—
are these words
these thoughts
held captive
cleverly packaged
neatly tucked
cynically shaped
I wonder
these words—
I wonder
these words—
that journey
from thought
to breath
where do they go

I wonder
are they kept
in a realm of
unspeakableness
like a
crippling tether?

I'VE LEARNED TO COUNT THE COST

Old trees now reign as landlord branches clutch
with curbs that cry and crumble from neglect
my childhood home is shattered window glass
and age-old memories thought to always last

City slick streets once populated with our summers
now silent weeds and waste become the renters
and dented doors of would-be legacy
are open wide to squat adversity

Oh how I long for what was always there
that sound and age of innocence so pure
would love to gather my emollient past
crushed sacred memories thought to always last

Sad state of affairs to see such ugliness
this once urban beauty thrived long ago
in vain I weep for what's forever lost
but now of age I've learned to count the cost.

TIME AND CHANCE

The race is not to the swift, nor the battle to the strong, neither yet bread to the wise, nor yet riches to men of understanding, nor yet favor to men of skill; but time and chance happens to them all.

Ecclesiastes 9:11 KJV

There are times when chances
are seen from a distance
down the street. Call it the
Race of Life. You can peer
with one eye, squint with
the other and know:

"This is going to be a
chance I have to take"

whether it lasts through
that moment, situation
or a lifetime it's exciting
by default because all the
anticipatory juices in the
world...don't know what
to expect when it happens
they just emerge, release
and come along for the ride.

SCATTERED PEARLS AND BROKEN GEMS

I wear a knotted necklace connecting unconnected thoughts
that vastly spiral around life's galaxy of social distance
I wear my scattered pearls of pensiveness and perplexity
I wear my broken gems of gendered lives seeking solace
clarity courage and understanding from life's crucible of
uncertainty and pandemonium.

SHEDDING

I am in a place of shedding the unwantedness
a place where I have nothing to lose because I
have lost everything. Everything that was supposed
to go. Shedding the unnecessary the unhealthy
the unpalatable. Shedding dead meaningless skin
the kind that comes off after you have stripped down
spa-soaked in hot warm cold water…yes landed
in a 110 degrees dry sauna room accompanied by
120 degrees steam room…then made your rounds
to a few more rooms of 150 degrees…inhaling
exhaling sweating cooling dehydrating
meditating journaling finally
by the time you are ready to complete
your renewal (without realizing it) your total body
especially your legs and feet (those vital parts
that carry you to and fro) have shed flakes and
flakes of unwanted unneeded dry dead skin from just
the slight... soothing… stroke of your slender fingers
and the experience itself
Yes, I am in a place of shedding…
loss may come but clarity will too and in time
I will learn what really matters. Much like
losing a loved one or close friend. Loss will
feel wretched when I release and shed…those
who know it feel it. You're devastated. The
pain befriends you. The hurt sustains you.
The grief rocks you. Days. Nights. But.
I learn to move on. I can get through this.
Whatever the THIS is.

GETTING UNSTUCK

I respond to things that move me: jolts music concerto
an art piece searing headlines a stunning even
despicable individual. Something small or minute
a soft voice maybe. Something that propels me
puts me back in my flow. My zone natural groove.
Could be a conversation or chance encounter with a
stranger. An intrinsic oftentimes spontaneous energy
that gets me moving moving out of my funk
flowing…flowing along to a place where life
becomes a dance again.

KNOT

I tie a string around my finger
reminding me not to be
reminded of everything
around me
tragically twisted
perniciously pious
politically pathetic

I won't get strung out
I tie a string around me
my whole body
my soul body
reminding me not to be
full of my remindedness.

VULNERABLE

These past five years
have been a balancing act:
each juggle has anchored
my arms 2000 miles apart
age and getting older—
that Great Equalizer
of it all
makes me realize I am
vulnerable to family
friends and life itself.

LAYING IT DOWN

I lay down all my sadness
collect my intersections and inner sections
finding natural ease joy tranquility like a
fluttering daffodil, dancing along fresh running
waters of a morning brook… rejoicing in every
chance encounter from my grandchild's smile.

THANK YOU'S

I am seated at a banqueting table of gratitude with
culled thank-you's for life and what it has taught
me, its covering an embellished cloth stitched from
swatches of memories and jewels toted in well-kept
luggage collected from vignettes of wisdom, episodes
of understanding, questions of curiosity that compel
my squinted eyes and desperate heart to wobble
through society's culture of civility, equity and dignity
igniting creative sparks of tenderness with empathy
reaped from love and loss transforming me to a place
of mindful meditation seeking a path that gives grace
and mercy to my evanescent soul.

A MOTHER'S FIRE

(Letter to a Grown Son)

I unleash these words and look at you
I ponder your path on this here earth
I know full well my heart concludes
how precious is your life and birth

survive the force that seeks to shake you
stay fixed on course never let it break you

I unleash these words and look at you
inside my own walls where I abide
from years and times on this here earth
my heart now filled with joy and pride

respond with confidence react not in fear
guard your choices stay humble my dear

I unleash this mighty breath of words
generational flames to light the way
so gird your soul and anchor your mind
with sparks of wisdom from day to day

know that some things must be proven
take my words for comfort and soothin'

I unleash these words with faith and love
a love bestowed from heaven above
what moves my heart is hope unseen
this fiery heirloom for you to glean.

V

GRANDCHILDREN

We arrive for playtime,
collective hearts feverish
for merriment
with scurrying feet
we head to a
cul de sac of discovery
where action heroes
hot-wheeled trucks lay
proudly scattered
red toy box awaiting
rambling fingers
five boys   one girl
victoriously   roam
crayons scrawl aimlessly
across make-believe
shapes   circles   squares
coins extemporaneously drop
from a chipped ceramic
piggy bank
floor time is a medley of
tumble   crawl   roll

run run run

you can't catch me

then together,
old bones and
young bones
we
all
fall
down.

WHEN I THINK ABOUT US

When I think about us
I smile with thanks
and beam with glee
to see God's work
on you and me
our precious talks
our daily chats
memories about this
news about that
though time has brought
much change indeed
we must respond
in time of need
When I think about us
I lift my legs to
run and dance
who would've thought
that time and chance
could teach the lessons
we both have learned
'been through the fire
and not get burned
my hands begin to
joyfully raise
I know God turns
heartache to praise
that's what I know
for sure to be
When I think about us –
just you and me.

WEEKENDS ARE MADE

I enjoy fresh sips of hot coffee, light buttered
pancakes, eggs over medium, side of bacon.
Water no ice. My mind is running. Gotta do
this...do that...

Weekends always get a raw deal.

Sure we live for them. Remember the tv jingle
"Weekends were made for Michelob."
Not everyone is a beer drinker or brewery enthusiast.
We use weekends as a dumping ground.
Time to do all the chores all the running around...
the stuff we couldn't do or get done during the week.
When I check out any major city these days, I find freeways
as busy on Saturday and Sunday as they
are on Tuesday and Friday.

Weekends are sacred. Downright precious.
Weekends are a special time. Time to relax,
kick back. Take the edge off. Place our hands
in our gardens, the rich soil. Feel that pulsing earth.
Take a drive to visit a loved one. A hurting one.
Attend a place of worship.

To worship the one who makes the soil for our
garden which helps our hands.
Our hands that hold our gifts from the earth,
from the soil, from the garden which helps our earth
which helps our hands connect with that luminous place
we call nature.
Yes, weekends don't just happen. They are made
and grown.

Downright special.

PASSION OF VEGETABLES

Robust designs by clever hands
lay host to culinary seeds made fertile
trim carrots blush while tomatoes flaunt
their shapely curves on outstretched vines
vidalia onions give sweet applause as
wet wild succulent beads from leafy lettuce
drip avidly down green grown leafy thighs
with open arms roasted garlic does tango
with parsley as steamed celery stalks gather
gazing like old men on a street corner.

WHY WE NEED CIVILITY

Life has become
an unusual flower
no longer remembering
the poise of lavender
kindness of mock orange
grace of calla lily

Life has become
a pernicious elixir
emitting rancid words
tossed like a young boy's
frisbee   stale thoughts
flung like bread pieces
to morning pigeons

Life has become
tension
like fear dangling
on a   tightrope

I pull   you pull
reciprocal winds
struggling to breathe.

EXCELLENCE IS IN YOUR GENES

As DNA reflects your traits
choices reflect your life
with the excellence that's inside of you
avoid unnecessary strife
put on a focused mindset
turn failure into gain
don't let these years on earth
pass frivolously in vain

Believe in every possibility
keep your mind rich with hope
life can be a lovely landscape
giving you the tools to help you cope
you'll face closed doors of opportunity
life's ups and downs will occur
let adversity renew your soul
while difficulties become a blur

You are not weak, you can achieve
despite how life may seem
take hold of all your worthiness
because excellence is in your genes

Spend quiet moments to stop and think
power off that cellphone EACH day
use that time to develop your thoughts
for your thoughts will guide your way

evaluate your needs and wants
don't let fear hold you back
study role models of success
stay steadfast, keep goals in tact
now as you analyze your thoughts
do the math...add it all up
may the sum of your precious thoughts
equal a river like an overflowing cup

for— you are not weak, you can achieve
despite how life may seem
you're blessed with God's greatest gift
Excellence is in your genes

Don't EVER hide your genius
trying to behave how others say
you only betray your inner gifts
thinking foolishness is the way
you can earn billions of money
you can gain world-wide fame
you can possess social media influence
where everybody knows your name
but the value of gaining WISDOM
is worth more than silver and gold
wise thoughts = wise steps
whether you're young or very old

You are not weak, you can achieve
despite how life may seem
so when situations challenge you
know that excellence is in your genes.

"Excellence is in Your Genes" was originally presented and read to the Graduating Class of 2025 Gateway Science Academy High School, St. Louis, Missouri. The poem was followed by this introduction:

"My dear graduates. I'd like for you to imagine that hidden inside those billions of neurons stored inside your brain, there's a special code that travels up and down the steps of your DNA ladder. So I challenge you right now and throughout your lifetime, to discover and tap into this remarkable support cell. This micro....tiny...but oh so powerful gene, I refer to as the EXCELLENCE gene—Yes, you have it! The ability to excel, to thrive, to soar."

AND STILL, WE SHINE

You may purge our past
fracture our future
with tainted toxic lies
you may cloud our goals with tear gas
rope our bodies stress our minds
but like the sun, we shine

You may spray engulfing flames of fear
prop your knees upon our neck
destroy our right to breathe—protest
you may saturate our neighborhoods
with drugs and rob us blind
but like the sun, we shine

Does our giftedness upset you
make you wish you had our minds?
cause we act like we've got greatness
flowing like money in summertime
just like jewels of rich red rubies
shining like precious emerald mines
all the brightly colored gems
Still.... we shine

Does our radiance upset you
does it take you for a loop?
that we speed like lustered pearls
like a bird in just one swoop
you may hide our untold stories
but we sparkle through shades of glories

your words may cut
your guns may spew
still our light will shine right through

Out of the mountains of justice
we shine
up from the skies of bitterness
we shine
we are young pearls, strong and mighty
iridescent in skill and quality
rich and rare but oh so great
outshining stones of age-old hate
bringing gifts of beauty and pride
we are the elders with our heads held high

We shine
We shine
We shine.

IMAGINE A WORLD

Imagine a world guided by a finely handled nib
etching calligraphic splendor on the tablets of

hearts transforming uncertainties pain unwanted
debris into clarity healing cleansing, like an unerring

balm soothing our homes our land our minds
cleansing our lens through which we see humanity

Let it come, let it heal.

Imagine a world imbued with grace and civility
where joy and courage are daily companions

of a grateful heart, wisdom is worn like a precious
necklace whose price is without measure, the voice

of fledgling birds sing morning melodies of
enchantment to its awakeners, street-keepers echo

kind words to ambivalent passerbys. Imagine a world
where the weak become strong, men no longer

nursed on breasts of helplessness and women whose self-
worth returns from a dormant vacation

children no longer playmates of misguidedness deception
and stolen innocence

whose companions now become strength and illumination

Let it come, let it enlighten.

Then, shall the seers of truth unmask our conceit
unveil our arrogance disrobe our inadequacies

leaving a world scented with crystal fragrant waters
washing the breaches, absorbing the affliction,

soothing utter sadness, casting fear down river cleansing our
hearts our earth anew

leaving hope rebirth, seeding new petals of possibility in
exchange

for the words we wear.

Let it come, let it flow.

ACKNOWLEDGMENTS

I would like to thank Dr. Rosetta T. Moore, Dorothy Lathan and the late Dr. Shirley Wilbert for their tremendous support and faith in my work as a poet, writer and individual.

To the St. Louis Poetry Center for providing me with an avenue and platform to nurture my poetic voice afterrelocating from Seattle, Washington to St. Louis, Missouri.

Abundant gratitude to my family and dear friends for their unwavering love and support. I am grateful for so much. To the memory of my parents whose courage, stability and quiet strength I cherish.

Thank you Jeanie Davies Okimoto (I am so grateful for your heartfelt investment in this project including your feedback, editorial suggestions and giving generously of your time) and the staff of Endicott and Hugh Books who gave their time and attention to these poems and its birth.

Bountiful thanks to everyone who encouraged and assisted me in bringing this collection to fruition!

ABOUT THE AUTHOR

Glendal Wallace is the author of two poetry collections, *Jewels of Fillmore* and *Unconnected Thoughts*. An educator and workshop presenter for over thirty-five years, she has published poetry, short stories and essays in many publications. Her writings appear in the anthology, *In Our Prime: Empowering Essays by Women on Love, Family, Career, Aging and Just Coping*, *Well Versed: The Literary Magazine of the Columbia Chapter of Missouri Writer's Guild* and other professional journals. She is a former board member of the St. Louis Poetry Center. Her main passion and commitment has been to inspire, encourage and educate writers at all levels. She lives with her family in St. Louis.

To learn more about what inspires her, visit poetryhealingstation.com.

www.ingramcontent.com/pod-product-compliance
Lightning Source LLC
LaVergne TN
LVHW090531110826
845146LV00003B/1062